# Needing Each Other

A Children's Book about Relational Needs

by

## Joy Wilt

**Illustrated by Ernie Hergenroeder**

Educational Products Division
Word, Incorporated
Waco, Texas

## Author

JOY WILT is creator and director of Children's Ministries, an organization that provides resources "for people who care about children"—speakers, workshops, demonstrations, consulting services, and training institutes. A certified elementary school teacher, administrator, and early childhood specialist, Joy is also consultant to and professor in the master's degree program in children's ministries for Fuller Theological Seminary. Joy is a graduate of LaVerne College, LaVerne, California (B.A. in Biological Science), and Pacific Oaks College, Pasadena, California (M.A. in Human Development). She is author of three books, *Happily Ever After*, *An Uncomplicated Guide to Becoming a Superparent*, and *Taming the Big Bad Wolves*, as well as the popular *Can-Make-And-Do Books*. Joy's commitment "never to forget what it feels like to be a child" permeates the many innovative programs she has developed and her work as lecturer, consultant, writer, and—not least—mother of two children, Christopher and Lisa.

## Artist

ERNIE HERGENROEDER is founder and owner of Hergie & Associates (a visual communications studio and advertising agency). With the establishment of this company in 1975, "Hergie" and his wife, Faith, settled in San Jose with their four children, Lynn, Kathy, Stephen, and Beth. Active in community and church affairs, Hergie is involved in presenting creative workshops for teachers, ministers, and others who wish to understand the techniques of communicating visually. He also lectures in high schools to encourage young artists toward a career in commercial art. Hergie serves as a consultant to organizations such as the Police Athletic League (PAL), Girl Scouts, and religious and secular corporations. His ultimate goal is to touch the hearts of kids (8 to 80) all over the world—visually!

ISBN 0-8499-8119-0
Library of Congress Catalog Card Number: 78-66146
Bruce Johnson, Editor

# Contents

# Introduction

<u>Needing Each Other</u> is one of a series of books.  The complete set is called  *Ready-Set-Grow!*

<u>Needing Each Other</u> deals with a child's emotional needs for love, respect, trust, and security. This book can be used by itself or as a part of a program that utilizes all of the *Ready-Set-Grow!* books.

<u>Needing Each Other</u> is specifically designed so that children can either read the book themselves or have it read to them.  This can be done at home, church, or school.  When reading to children, it is not necessary to complete the book at one sitting.  Concern should be given to the attention span of the individual child and his or her comprehension of the subject matter.

<u>Needing Each Other</u> is designed to involve the child in the concepts that are being taught.  This is done by simply and carefully explaining each concept and then asking questions that invite a response from the child.  It is hoped that by answering the questions the child will personalize the concept and, thus, integrate it into his or her thinking.

Every person has within himself or herself the resources to give to other people, and receive from them; love, respect, trust, and security. These needs must be understood and dealt with if the person is to survive and grow.

Needing Each Other explains how a child can get his or her emotional needs met in acceptable ways. Situations and examples are given to help the child recognize and respect the importance of feelings in others and in himself or herself.

Needing Each Other is designed to teach children the importance of respect and love. Emphasis is placed on the child as an individual with unique physical, mental, and emotional traits that can only be recognized and enhanced through the love and respect of others. This book is also designed to teach a child that when God created him or her, God did not make any mistakes. Everything God does has a purpose and fits into a total plan. "Loving and giving" are a part of God's plan for every human being. Children who grow up believing and accepting this will be equipped to live healthy, exciting lives.

# Needing Each Other

God created you a person, and because you are one . . .

you have special needs.

**A person needs . . .**

good food, water, air, sunshine, exercise, rest, sleep, clothes, and shelter in order to keep his or her body alive and well.

Persons were also created by God to need other people.

Why is this true?

Well, to begin with . . .

# Chapter 1

# A Person Needs to Love Others

**What does it mean to love others?**

This is Karen.

Karen's favorite toy is her teddy bear.
Karen loves her teddy bear.

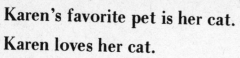

Karen's favorite pet is her cat.

Karen loves her cat.

Karen's best friend is Michele.
Karen loves Michele.

What does it mean to say that

Karen loves her teddy bear,
Karen loves her cat, and
Karen loves Michele?

It means that Karen values her teddy bear, cat, and best friend. They are very important to her. They mean a lot to her.

Because Karen values her teddy bear, and because
it is important to her . . .

she takes time to care for it.

Karen shares her bed with her teddy bear and always
sees that it gets repaired when it gets damaged.

Because Karen values her cat, and because she is important to her . . .

Karen takes time to care for her.

Karen shares her best doll bed and blankets with the cat, and often spends some of her allowance to buy cat toys and catnip for her.

Because Karen values her best friend, Michele, and because
Michele means so much to her . . .

Karen spends time with Michele.

Karen helps Michele with her jobs and shares her things with her.

Because Karen loves her teddy bear, her cat, and best friend, Michele,

she spends time with them,
she does things for them, and
she shares her things with them.

If you love someone,

> you will value him or her,
> he or she will be important to you, and
> he or she will mean a lot to you.

If you love someone,

> you will spend time with him or her,
> you will do things for him or her, and
> you will share your things with him or her.

God created you with a need to love others.  God wants
you to love others.

Who are some of the people you love?

_____

_____

Why does a person need other people?

# Chapter 2

# A Person Needs to Be Loved by Others

**What does it mean to be loved by others?**

This is John.

These are John's parents.

John's parents love him.

This is John's next-door neighbor Mr. Stevens.

Mr. Stevens loves John.

This is John's best friend, Chris.

Chris loves John.

**What does it mean to say that**

John's parents love John,
Mr. Stevens loves John, and
Chris loves John?

It means that they value John. John
is very important to them. John means
a lot to them.

Because John's parents value John, and because he is important to them . . .

they care for him.

John's parents spend time with him and they share their money, home, and other things with him.

Because Mr. Stevens values John, and because John is important to him . . .

he spends time with John and does things for him like fixing John's bike.

Mr. Stevens shares his things with John.

Because Chris values John, and because John is
important to him . . .

he spends time with John and helps him with
his arithmetic homework.

Chris shares his things with John.

Because John's parents, his neighbor Mr. Stevens, and his best friend, Chris, love him,

> they spend time with him,
> they do things for him, and
> they share their things with him.

If someone loves you,

 he or she will value you,
 you will be important to him or her, and
 you will mean a lot to him or her.


If someone loves you,

 he or she will spend time with you,
 he or she will do things for you, and
 he or she will share his or her things with you.


God created you with a need to be loved by others. God
wants you to be loved by others.


Who are some of the people that love you?

_____

_____

**This is Carolyn.**

Carolyn says that nobody loves her.

If this is true . . .

Carolyn is the only one who can do something about it.

The answer is simple.  In order to be loved, you must do two things.

First, if you want another person to love you, you must love yourself. You must realize that God created and loves you, and because of this, you are special.  Because you are a special person created and loved by God, you should love yourself.

Second, if you want another person to love you, you must love him or her. You must realize that God created and loves that person, and because of this, he or she is special.  Because he or she is a special person created and loved by God, you should love him or her.

**Every person needs to love others and be loved by others.**

Why does a person need other people?

# Chapter 3

# A Person Needs to Respect Others

# What does it mean to respect others?

This is Hope.

This is Hope's mother.

Hope respects her mother.

This is Hope's teacher, Mr. Berry.

Hope respects Mr. Berry.

This is Hope's best friend, Rebecca.

Hope respects Rebecca.

**What does it mean to say that**

Hope respects her mother,
Hope respects Mr. Berry, and
Hope respects Rebecca?

It means that Hope admires her mother,
Mr. Berry, and Rebecca. She thinks good
things about them. She thinks they are
OK just the way they are.

Even though some people criticize her mother . . .

Hope admires her mother. Hope thinks her mother
is OK just the way she is.

Even though some people criticize a lot of things
about Mr. Berry . . .

Hope admires Mr. Berry.

She thinks that Mr. Berry
is OK just the way he is.

Even though some people criticize a lot of things
about Rebecca . . .

Hope admires Rebecca. She thinks that Rebecca is OK just the way she is.

Because Hope respects her mother, her teacher,
Mr. Berry, and her best friend, Rebecca,

    she admires them,
    she thinks good things about them, and
    she thinks that they are OK just the way they are.

If you respect someone,

    you will admire him or her,
    you will think good things about him or her, and
    you will think that he or she is OK just the way he or she is.

God created you with a need to respect others.  God wants you to respect others.

Who are some of the people you respect?

_____

_____

Why does a person need other people?

# Chapter 4

## A Person Needs to Be Respected by Others

# What does it mean to be respected by others?

This is David.

This is David's father.

David's father respects him.

This is David's soccer coach, Mr. Thomas.

Mr. Thomas respects David.

This is David's friend Eugene.

Eugene respects David.

What does it mean to say that

David's father respects David,
Mr. Thomas respects David, and
Eugene respects David?

It means that they admire David. They think good things about him and think that he is OK just the way he is.

Even though other people criticize David . . .

I DON'T UNDERSTAND WHAT HAPPENED TO DAVID. HIS DAD WAS AN ALL-STAR BALL PLAYER.

David's father admires him and thinks that David is OK just the way he is.

Even though other people criticize David . . .

Mr. Thomas admires him and thinks David is OK just the way he is.

**Even though other people criticize David . . .**

Eugene admires David and thinks David is
OK just the way he is.

Because David's father, his coach Mr. Thomas, and his friend Eugene respect him,

they admire him,
they think good things
about him, and
they think that
David is OK just the
way he is.

If someone respects you,

> he or she will admire you,
> he or she will think good things about you, and
> he or she will think that you are OK just the way you are.

God created you with a need to be respected by others. God wants you to be respected by others.

Who are some of the people who respect you?

_____

_____

**This is Harold.**

**Harold says that nobody respects him.**

If this is true . . .

Harold is the only one who can do something about it.

The answer is simple. In order to be respected, you must do two things.

First, if you want another person to respect you, you must respect yourself. You must realize that God created and respects you and because of this, you are special. Because you are a special person created and respected by God, you should respect yourself.

Second, if you want another person to respect you, you must respect him or her. You must realize that God created and respects that person, and because of this, he or she is special. Because he or she is a special person created and respected by God, you should respect him or her.

Every person must respect others and be respected by others.

Why does a person need other people?

# Chapter 5

## A Person Needs to Trust Others

**What does it mean to trust others?**

This is Raymond.

These are Raymond's grandparents.

Raymond trusts his grandparents.

**These are Raymond's friends, Jack and Tom.**

Raymond trusts Jack and Tom.

**What does it mean to say that**

Raymond trusts his grandparents,
Raymond trusts Jack, and
Raymond trusts Tom?

It means that Raymond can depend on his
grandparents and his friends, Jack and Tom.
He knows that they are honest, unselfish, and
fair.

**Because Raymond trusts his grandparents . . .**

he can always depend on them.

He knows that they
do what they say
they will do.

**Because Raymond trusts his grandparents . . .**

WE WOULD HAVE BEEN HERE EARLIER, BUT WE WERE OUTSIDE GARDENING AND COMPLETELY LOST TRACK OF THE TIME.

He knows that they are honest.

He knows that what they say to him is true.

WE WANTED TO GIVE YOU
SOMETHING FOR HELPING
US CLEAN OUR
GARAGE
LAST
WEEK.

He knows that they are unselfish and fair. 99

Because Raymond trusts Jack and Tom . . .

He can always depend on them.

He knows that they will do what they say they will do.

Because Raymond trusts
Jack and Tom . . .

102

he knows that they are honest. He knows that
what they say to him is true.

SINCE WE HAD
THE CAMP-OUT IN
YOUR BACKYARD, WE
THOUGHT THAT IT
WOULD ONLY BE
FAIR FOR US TO
BRING THE SNACKS!

Raymond knows that they are unselfish and fair.

Because Raymond trusts his grandparents and his friends Jack and Tom,

> he can depend on them,
> he knows that they are honest, and
> he knows that they are unselfish and fair.

YOU KNOW, THE FOUR PEOPLE I LIKE MOST BESIDES YOU ARE GRANDMA, GRANDPA, JACK, AND TOM. I GUESS IT'S BECAUSE I CAN TRUST THEM.

If you trust someone,

    you can depend on him or her,
you know that he or she will be honest, and
you know that he or she will be unselfish and fair.

God created you with a need to trust others. God wants you to trust others.

Who are some of the people you trust?

_____

_____

**Why does a person need others?**

# Chapter 6

# A Person Needs to Be Trusted by Others

# What does it mean to be trusted by others?

This is Linda.

These are Linda's parents.

Linda's parents trust her.

These are Linda's friends Laura and Pete.

Laura and Pete trust Linda.

What does it mean to say that

Linda's parents trust Linda,
Laura trusts Linda, and
Pete trusts Linda?

It means that they can depend on Linda. They know that she is honest. They know that she is unselfish and fair.

**Because Linda'a parents trust Linda . . .**

they can depend on her. They know that she is honest.

**Linda's parents know that she is unselfish and fair.**

MRS. GREEN STOPPED ME ON THE WAY HOME FROM SCHOOL TODAY AND GAVE ME THIS BAG OF COOKIES. SHE BAKED THEM TODAY. WANT SOME?

**Because Laura and Pete trust Linda . . .**

I WAS DISAPPOINTED THAT MOM WOULDN'T LET US USE THE INDIAN POTTERY FOR OUR REPORT, BUT SHE DID SAY THAT WE COULD USE THE INDIAN ARROWHEADS AND DOLLS, AND I REMEMBERED TO BRING THOSE.

they can depend on her. They know that she is honest.

Laura and Pete know that Linda is unselfish and fair.

117

Because Linda's parents and her friends Laura and Pete trust her,

they can depend on her,
they know that she is honest, and
they know that she is unselfish and fair.

If someone trusts you,

> he or she can depend on you,
> he or she knows that you will be honest, and
> he or she knows that you will be unselfish and fair.

God created you with a need to be trusted by others. God wants you to be trusted by others.

Who are some of the people who trust you?

_____

_____

This is Marvin.

Marvin says that nobody trusts him.

If this is true . . .

Marvin is the only one who can do something about it.

The answer is simple. In order to be trusted, you must do two things.

First, if you want another person to trust you, you must show that you can be trusted. You must be dependable (do what you say you will do), honest (say what is true), unselfish, and fair. You must be trustworthy.

Second, if you want another person to trust you, you must trust the other person. You must trust that he or she will be dependable, honest, unselfish, and fair. You must trust someone else.

**Every person needs to trust others and be trusted by others.**

So why does a person need other people?

## Conclusion

You are a person created by God, and because you are one, you need

    to love others,
    to be loved by others,

    to respect others,
    to be respected by others,

    to trust others, and
    to be trusted by others.

That is why . . .

People need each other.